Enjoy the Water

Contents | Page

written by John Lockyer

Do you like to have fun in water?
Do you like to play in a creek, a lake, a river, or the sea?

You can go under the water. You can make bubbles and you can kick with two fins.

If you have goggles then you might see some fish. If the fish swim by, they will look big.

To go down deep in the water, you need a tank on your back. You can swim in and out of a shipwreck.

You can have lots of fun in rapids. You can dash over rocks, logs, and drop offs.

kayaking

In rapids, you can spin, roll, hop, twist and turn, too. You might get dizzy and tip out!

rafting

surfing

To catch a wave, you need to be quick. You can go up the wave and then come down.

When it is hot, you can stand up and float on the water. You will enjoy it if there is no wind.

paddle boarding

If the wind blows then you might enjoy this water sport. If you are good you can jump, spin, and flip.

windsurfing

This is a water sport for the wind, too. The water will have waves and many bumps and lumps.

Sit down. Look up. Feel the grips.
When you hear, 'Go!', pull hard.
Pull very hard and you will go fast.

Hit the drum. Boom! Hit the drum. Boom! When you hear that you will dip down into the water and pull fast.

dragon boating

You need to be fit for this water sport. You can kick, swim, and dive to get the ball.

When you get the ball, hold it in one hand. Then toss it very hard. It might go in. Goal!

Water is fun! We can be in it, on it, or under it. Lots of us enjoy the water.

swimming